Rache Mysterious Drawings

Richard Brown
Illustrated by Gary Taylor

CAMBRIDGE
UNIVERSITY PRESS

Cambridge Reading

General Editors
Richard Brown and Kate Ruttle

Consultant Editor
Jean Glasberg

PUBLISHED BY THE PRESS SYNDICATE OF THE UNIVERSITY OF CAMBRIDGE
The Pitt Building, Trumpington Street, Cambridge CB2 1RP, United Kingdom

CAMBRIDGE UNIVERSITY PRESS
The Edinburgh Building, Cambridge CB2 2RU, United Kingdom
40 West 20th Street, New York, NY 10011-4211, USA
10 Stamford Road, Oakleigh, Melbourne 3166, Australia

First published 1998

Printed in the United Kingdom at the University Press, Cambridge

Typeset in Concorde

A catalogue record for this book is available from the British Library

ISBN 0 521 63947 6 paperback

**Other Cambridge Reading books
you may enjoy**

Ollie
Irene Yates

Captain Cool and the Ice Queen
Gerald Rose

Garlunk
Helen Cresswell

**Other books by Richard Brown
you may enjoy**

How to Trick a Tiger

The Midnight Party

1

Rachel's day at school seemed to get longer and longer, like a stretched elastic band, and she was almost at breaking point when she finally escaped across the playground. She'd had a rotten day – everything had been too hard, too noisy, too hurtful – and as she walked towards her mum she hunched her shoulders and scowled deeply inside herself.

"Ratty," thought Mum. She knew better than to ask what the matter was; it would come out in time. "OK, love?"

Rachel nodded, barely lifting her gaze from the pavement. Some days sang in your head, others just screeched. She kicked a stone, viciously.

At home, after a glass of milk and a chocolate biscuit, the scowl inside her softened a bit – but not much. She sat in a big armchair in the studio and watched as Mum flicked on an Anglepoise lamp above a drawing board. Mum was a picture-book artist and spent her day drawing and painting.

"I've just about finished this picture," she said after a long, ticking silence. "Want to have a look?"

Rachel shook her head. She *did* want to look, but the scowl inside her wouldn't let her.

"You *have* had a bad day, haven't you," said Mum. "Anything in particular?"

Rachel shook her head again – words were too much effort. And besides, there *was* nothing in particular.

Mum often drew her daughter; it was her equivalent of taking photographs. She had a whole album of such sketches. She took a sheet of paper and a pencil and began to draw.

Out of the pencil came a scowling, bad-tempered, ratty little girl that made Mum laugh.

This time Rachel came over to look. Yes, that was exactly how she felt. The clenched fists, the blazing eyes, the foot about to stamp. "Can I keep it, Mum?" she asked.

That night, she went to bed early, feeling tired and headachy. She propped the drawing up beside her bedside lamp. She tried outstaring the girl in the drawing, willing her to be happy. But Rachel's eyelids grew heavy and soon she fell asleep. Mum came in to turn out the light.

2

Rachel woke to a strange sound. A little
rattle, a brief pause, a click of something
hitting a surface, then a snigger. This was
repeated several times. There was a little
glow of ghostly light. Rachel blinked,
then blinked harder; she felt frightened.

Whatever was that sitting on her
toy-box?

It looked like a ghostly little girl with
a scowling face – or like a little sketch

of one. The little sketch-girl started to
rummage in a box of Lego. Pulling out a
brick, she hurled it against the wardrobe,
then giggled and dipped into the box for
another brick.

She saw Rachel staring at her.

She stuck out her tongue at Rachel as if
to say, "Who do you think you're staring
at?" She hurled a brick that hit Rachel on
the chin.

"Ouch!" Rachel ducked under the
covers. More bricks sailed past her head.
Then they stopped.

When Rachel looked again, the ghostly little girl was at the bottom of her bed, pulling a weird face at her. "Go away," said Rachel rather feebly.

With a laugh, the figure jumped off the bed, floated down to the floor, and ran out of the bedroom.

Rachel listened fearfully. There were strange sounds coming from the bathroom. Glugging sounds. Tearing sounds. Sniggers and giggles. And sounds she couldn't identify.

She listened. She watched the door . . .

Then all went silent.

11

3

In the morning, Rachel was woken by the telephone ringing. Mum got out of bed to answer it.

"It's Grandad," she called. "He's spending a day at the lake. Do you want to go with him?"

"Yes, please," said Rachel, eagerly jumping out of bed.

But she nearly didn't make it to the lake. When Mum discovered the mess in the bathroom, they both looked at it in silent disbelief. She *knew* she hadn't done it . . . Or had she, in her sleep?

She had to work hard to clean it up. As she mopped and wiped, she tried to work out what had happened. It was all so puzzling . . . She was thinking so hard that she almost forgot Grandad was coming to take her out.

4

Grandad took her hand and led her along
a wooded path to the hide where you sat
with binoculars and watched birds on the
lake. A sign said, *Please Keep Quiet*, but
today, Rachel was full of words – she had
hardly stopped talking since Grandad had
picked her up in his car.

"You're cheerful today," Grandad
chuckled.

Now, as they stepped into the shadowy hide, she had to keep her teeth firmly clamped together to stop the words coming out and scaring the birds away.

She saw moorhens and ducks and loud geese. She trained Grandad's binoculars on one lone swan and followed it as it drifted along the lake's edge. The curve of its folded wings was perfect in the still light. That made her feel peaceful at last: the remains of yesterday's scowl, which had clung to her insides like a line of grime around the bath, had at last dissolved.

They ate a picnic leaning against a tree.
The silver-grey water lapped against the
bank below them. Its soft, rhythmic sound
lulled Grandad into a doze.

Rachel sat very still. Occasionally, the
water plopped as if there were big fish just
under the surface.

Her mind went back to the mysterious events of the previous night. The strange dream of the ghostly girl, just like her mum's sketch of her . . . And then to the mess in the bathroom – talc all over the floor, the toilet roll unravelled, the toothpaste squirted around the sink, the puddles of shampoo. Rachel felt hurt at being accused of making the mess. It wasn't fair!

It was warm by the lake and she was growing drowsy. She was just about to doze off like Grandad when she heard a sound in the water below her. Peering over the edge of the bank, she saw a sleek, brown animal the size of a large cat slip into the water. She watched it spellbound. The animal, its head and eyes just showing above the rippling water, swam in a wide arc, then returned to the bank further down where it disappeared.

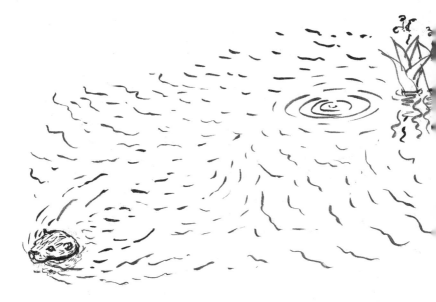

"Grandad!" Rachel shouted, waking him from his doze. "I think I've just seen an otter!"

Grandad was struck by the happy look on her face, the shine of light in her eyes. "That was special," he said. "They're such shy creatures. Pretty rare, too. They don't show themselves to just anyone, you know."

5

They got back to Grandad's in time for tea.

After they'd eaten, Grandad opened a drawing pad and selected a pencil. "You sit quietly there, miss," he said. "I'm going to capture that grin on your face."

"Can *you* draw then, Grandad?" She knew he could but this was a little game they often played.

"Can *I* draw?" Grandad echoed in mock disgust. "What a cheek! Who do you think taught your mum to draw, then?"

"Don't know," said Rachel with a laugh.

"I did, of course. I drew her sitting in that chair, just as I'm drawing you now. Fancy you not knowing that."

Grandad drew, and Rachel thought of the otter. When he had finished, she could see that every line he had drawn had exactly captured the day's happy mood.

6

Just before bed that night, Mum
complained about the mess in Rachel's
room. Clothes everywhere, toys scattered
about, books in heaps, crayons broken
and ground into the carpet. "It's not *like*
you, Rachel."

Rachel could only stare at it all in dismay. By now she was pretty sure who had made the mess. But she knew Mum wouldn't believe her. She could hardly believe it herself. It was so unfair!

"You'd better not make a habit of this," Mum warned, helping her to tidy up.

Tucking Rachel into bed, Mum said, "Do you *remember* going into the bathroom last night and making that mess?"

Rachel shook her head. Mum knew her daughter better than anyone and she could see that Rachel was telling the truth, or what the child thought was the truth. Had she started sleepwalking, then, or had she just forgotten? She kissed Rachel goodnight.

Rachel had put Grandad's sketch of her next to Mum's sketch. It was probably a trick of the dim light, but it seemed to her as if the girls in both drawings were now facing each other, as if they were squaring up to each other.

She suddenly thought: Why don't I *rub out* Mum's drawing? That'll get rid of that bad-tempered little girl.

She climbed out of bed, found a rubber, and began to rub out the pencil lines, starting with one of the slippers. She rubbed out most of the slipper before she had to stop. Little prickles, like pins and needles, ran up her arm. And the girl in the sketch wasn't just scowling now, she was outraged! "How dare you? How *dare* you?" she screeched, dancing about with one slipper off, one slipper on. Rachel dropped the rubber and shot back into bed.

7

In the night she heard them arguing.

"*I* should stay. I'm the one she likes,"
said Grandad's picture of the happy girl.

"Yes, but she can't be happy every day,"
said Mum's picture of the scowling girl.
"No-one is. She needs me too."

"She doesn't need you. She hates you. She's scared of what you might do next."

"That's as it should be. If she liked me, there'd be no hope for her, would there?"

"Well then, perhaps we should *both* stay," said the happy girl after a pause.

"What? You expect me to put up with *you* every day? No way!"

"In that case, neither of us should stay. We could go and sit in that album of her mum's with all the other drawings."

The scowling girl thought about this for a while. "Nope," she said at last. "Rachel would be such a dull little girl if we did that, wouldn't she? And besides, I'd die of boredom in that album."

"It's either you or me, then," said the happy girl, her voice very determined.

Suddenly they were rolling about in a sort of paper wrestling match all over the carpet and among the Lego. The fight got faster and more furious until everything was a whirling ball and a blur . . .

8

In the morning, both sketches had gone from Rachel's bedside. There were a couple of scrappy bits of paper on the floor, very creased and a bit torn, but no drawings.

"Mum," she said, coming into the studio. "Have you taken that drawing you did of me in a bad mood? And Grandad's too?"

Mum shook her head. "You haven't lost them, have you?"

Rachel shrugged. "They've disappeared," she said.

"I'll draw you another one," said Mum, seeing how puzzled her daughter looked.

Rachel sat there while her mother drew. Snatches of the conversation she had dreamed of last night strayed back into her head, but they did not make much sense.

She didn't mind that the scowling sketch had disappeared, but where was the happy one?

The new drawing exactly caught the mix of her moods. "This one," she said, "is *really* me. I'll hang it in my room."

But that isn't quite the end of the story. Sometimes Rachel fancies she can hear a soft singing in the dark. It seems to come from the picture hanging on her wall. It makes her feel happy.

At other times she fancies she can hear a faint, bad-tempered, ratty little voice, saying, "Where's my slipper? I want my slipper. *Give me back my slipper!*"
And that always makes Rachel laugh.